THAMES PLEASURE STEAMERS
from 1945

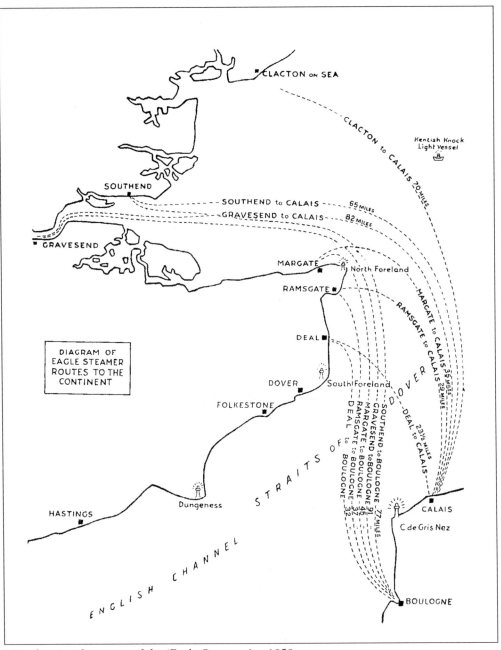

Map showing the routes of the 'Eagle Steamers', c.1959.

THAMES PLEASURE STEAMERS
from 1945

Andrew Gladwell

*This book is dedicated to the late Bill Gladwell who gave me my interest in the
London River*

TEMPUS

First published 2001
Copyright © Andrew Gladwell, 2001

Tempus Publishing Limited
The Mill, Brimscombe Port,
Stroud, Gloucestershire, GL5 2QG
www.tempus-publishing.com

ISBN 0 7524 2351 7

Typesetting and origination by
Tempus Publishing Limited
Printed in Great Britain by
Midway Colour Print, Wiltshire

The *Waverley* looking magnificent as she departs from Great Yarmouth on 12 August 2000 to undertake trials after her rebuild.

Contents

Eagle Steamers

Brochure from 1966 showing the three 'Eagle Steamer' motor vessels that are remembered with great fondness by so many.

Acknowledgements

In compiling this book, I have appreciated the generosity of the individuals below who have given so much time to ensure that the heritage of Thames pleasure steamers is preserved. A great deal of the material in this book comes from the Paddle Steamer Preservation Society Collection and is being shown here for the first time. My thanks must therefore go to Nick James and the PSPS for investing resources to ensure that this important maritime collection survives for future generations. Many people have been generous with their time and material and I would like to thank Glasgow University Archives Service, Dr Joe McKendrick, Walter Bowie, Alan Bruce, Ellie Newlands, Rev. Norman Bird, Waverley Excursions Ltd, Mike Schooley, Jean Spells, Patrick Taylor, Stuart Cameron, Ray Palmer Collection, Paddle Steamer Kingswear Castle Trust, Tom Lee, Marjorie Fuller, Roddy McKee, Marion Bowyer, Peter Stocker, Philip Kershaw, John Goss, Richard Danielson, Alex Duncan, Alec Ramage and Arthur Rickner. Three people deserve special mention: Peter Box, the foremost expert on Thames paddle steamers, has been invaluable during the compilation of this book and has, over the years, imparted his enthusiasm and great interest. Secondly, Robin Toy has been of great assistance and has allowed me to use the collection of his late father Jim Toy, who worked for GSNC for many happy years. Lastly, I would like to say a very special 'thank you' to John Richardson MBE who has allowed me to use his unique material which captures so vividly the great days of the 'Eagle Steamers'. To all of these individuals I extend my thanks.

Introduction

To a generation of Londoners the trip aboard a paddle steamer to the seaside was a traditional and essential part of life each summer. By the 1930s sleek new pleasure steamers, luxuriously appointed and reflecting a new age, were being introduced to gradually replace the older paddle steamers; the future therefore seemed assured. There was an air of confidence that the pattern of life for millions of Londoners would not change. However, the Second World War left scars that dealt these traditional and well-loved vessels a major blow. Some vessels witnessed what might have been their greatest hour as they swapped their usual cargo of daytrippers for troops rescued during the miracle of Dunkirk. Others did not survive and the gleaming new vessels *Royal Sovereign* and *Queen of the Channel* joined the old favourite *Crested Eagle* as fatalities of war. The fleet of 1945 was a mere shadow of its former self with only six vessels returning from a pre-war figure of thirteen. With the cessation of hostilities in 1945 no time was lost in getting the fleet ready again. So, on 8 June 1946, *Royal Eagle* sailed again, signalling that normality had returned to the Thames. *Golden Eagle* followed in 1947, followed shortly afterwards by the splendid *Royal Daffodil* and the Dunkirk heroine, *Medway Queen*. The sheer confidence in the future of Thames pleasure steamers was reflected in the building of the magnificent *Royal Sovereign* in 1948 and the *Queen of the Channel* in 1949; both built to replace wartime losses. By the close of the 1940s, the stage was set for what might have been a new 'Golden Age' of relaxation and enjoyment on the Thames.

These much-loved vessels were 'special' for many reasons. For many they conjure up visions of people singing and dancing to the happy tune of the accordion; Pearly Kings and Queens often strolled along the decks; the famous wit of the many cockneys aboard enjoying an all too rare day out and day-trippers wore their novelty hats from Southend. Alongside this carnival of merriment was a more sedate side. These were indeed luxurious motor vessels and offered the very best in accommodation, service and speed. Wide spacious decks, enormous dining saloons capable of serving over 1,300 meals a day, with the opportunity of having afternoon tea served by a liveried steward, made these vessels the ultimate in luxury. They were indeed 'London's Luxury Liners'.

The Second World War had changed so much of life in Britain. The 'Peoples War' had changed attitudes and this was reflected dramatically in the years that followed. By the early 1950s, the *Royal Eagle* and *Golden Eagle* were withdrawn, leaving the three young motor vessels to carry on the tradition. This decline in trade was caused mainly by the increasing popularity of the family motorcar. The Paid Holidays Act of 1948 had also opened up the amount of time available for relaxation. Now, instead of having just one day trip or two a year, people were taking longer holidays of a week or more. They were also becoming more adventurous as they ventured further afield than Margate or Southend; perhaps to one of the new holiday camps or indeed even on a package tour abroad. With these considerations and the added burden of high maintenance costs, the death knell was indeed sounding for the Thames pleasure steamers.

The 1950s saw the beginning of a programme of scrapping almost every paddle and pleasure steamer around the UK. Heritage had no place in 1950s Britain and the charming reminders of a gentler age found their way to the scrapyard. Even the once mighty General Steam Navigation Company (or 'Eagle Steamers' are they were more commonly known) fell victim to the decline. By the early 1960s, the pace of withdrawal was reaching a crescendo; famous and much loved vessels disappeared one after another amid great emotion and despair.

In 1959, the Paddle Steamer Preservation Society was formed with the aim of halting this decline; alas, there was little that could be done. In 1963 the popular *Medway Queen* was withdrawn amid great public outcry and was eventually saved for preservation. On 20 December 1966 the General Steam Navigation Company announced that the three much loved Thames motor vessels were to be sold. The long and happy tradition of a pleasure cruise by 'Eagle Steamers' to the sea was at an end.

Throughout the 1960s, attempts were made to re-introduce pleasure steamer trips. In 1963 the famous Victorian *Consul* spent a short time on the Thames in an attempt to run a paddle steamer service. In 1966 the ex-Clyde paddle steamer *Jeanie Deans* was lavishly refitted and renamed *Queen of the South* for service on the Thames. Sadly, serious mechanical problems curtailed her season drastically and similar problems beset her in 1967. This brought what might have been a significant step in continuing the heritage of paddle steamers to a sudden and unhappy end. They were all valiant early attempts at preservation in an era when 'heritage' was not a marketable product.

For eleven years the Thames was still to the happy throng of daytrippers. However, over four hundred miles away on the Clyde, a miracle was happening. The *Waverley* had spent her career rather anonymously fulfilling the duties for which she had entered service in 1947 but the early 1970s saw her 'uniqueness' as the last sea-going paddle steamer in the world recognised as significant. Heritage and a fascination with the past were at last awakening. Her sale in 1973 for £1 and her subsequent career has been astounding. By 1977, it was felt that a viable financial market might be found away from the Firth of Clyde. In April 1978 *Waverley* swept majestically under the raised bascules of Tower Bridge – a paddle steamer service was once again a feature of the Thames, much to the delight of those that remembered the old days and to the wonder of new enthusiasts. Since that time *Waverley* has indeed become as much loved as the famous 'Eagle Steamers' and each year recreates the classic cruises of the past. In 1987 her consort *Balmoral* joined her on visits to the London River. Another annual visitor is the wonderful coal-fired *Kingswear Castle* built originally for the River Dart in Devon.

The years since 1946 have seen perhaps the most dramatic events ever in the distinguished history of Thames paddle and pleasure steamers. From the confidence of 'Eagle Steamers' in 1946 to the sad and dramatic loss of the three motor vessels, a phoenix has risen from the ashes in the form of *Waverley*, *Balmoral* and *Kingswear Castle*. In the twenty-first century we are indeed privileged to enjoy the relaxed and simple atmosphere of a pleasure steamer cruise to the sea – a cruise so beloved by generations that have lived alongside the London River.

One
Royal Eagle & Golden Eagle

The *Royal Eagle* was built for service on the Thames in 1932. The vessel had re-entered service on the first anniversary of VE Day in 1946. She soon settled into her regular service from London to Southend and Margate. Her master at this time was Capt. Traynier.

The *Royal Eagle* leaving Southend in 1949. In this year 278,655 passengers used the pleasure steamers at Southend Pier with many enjoying a cruise to see the famous illuminations which lit up the promenade in the autumn.

The deck lounge aboard the *Royal Eagle*. This lounge was 150ft in length and was comfortably furnished with Lloyd Loom armchairs and tables. Often on the return journey, a tea dance was held to music broadcast over the ship's loudspeaker system.

The cocktail bar aboard the *Royal Eagle*. This 'Olde Time' smoking room provided a 'popular retreat for gentlemen passengers'.

The *Royal Eagle* was built for comfort. On her main deck she had both a First and Second Class dining saloon, several bars and a number of private dining rooms (towards the stern) that could be hired to accommodate up to fourteen people or, if combined, a larger group.

The *Royal Eagle* at Southend Pier, *c.*1948.

On a vessel such as the *Royal Eagle*, the catering crew might number seventy. In a day they might serve 300 breakfasts and 1,000 lunches and high teas. Catering stores were loaded onto the ship between 6 a.m. and 8 a.m. during which time an average of ten tons of stores were loaded. This included meat, vegetables, beer, soft drinks and ices. As food was still in short supply after the war, the Ministry of Food issued a special licence. Records were kept of everything consumed aboard the *Royal Eagle* as the Ministry based their allowance on the Company's returns.

The *Golden Eagle* was built in 1909 by John Brown & Co. of Clydebank and became a firm favourite with passengers. After the Second World War, she re-entered service in 1947 and was placed on the run from London to Southend and Clacton. Capt. Kitto commanded her during this period. She was withdrawn after the 1949 season. Shortly afterwards, P&A Campbell discussed with the General Steam Navigation Company the possibility of operating either *Golden Eagle* or *Royal Eagle* out of Brighton. However, this idea was soon abandoned resulting in the *Golden Eagle* being sent for scrapping in the middle of 1951.

The *Royal Eagle* arrives at Southend Pier in 1949.

Southend Pier in 1949. At this time the pier was incredibly popular with five million visitors in 1949 alone. Most passengers disembarking from a pleasure steamer rode on one of the new streamlined trains to visit the famous Kursaal or the amusements on the promenade. Others dined in the Dolphin Restaurant or were serenaded by Ben Oakley and his Orchestra at the Pier Head.

The *Royal Eagle* was withdrawn from service in 1950 and laid up close to Upnor on the River Medway. It took another three years before she was refloated on an exceptionally high tide. She was then taken to Grays for breaking up.

Another photograph from January 1954 showing the *Royal Eagle* about to embark upon her final journey.

Eight year old Brian Jessup is seen standing against the paddle box of the *Royal Eagle* whilst she awaited demolition *c.*1952.

The funnel of the *Royal Eagle* awaiting scrapping. The General Steam Navigation Company emblem can be clearly seen on the side.

A sad sight as the engines of the *Royal Eagle* lie in a mangled mess in the scrapyard at Grays. The once mighty three-cylinder main engine had driven the 25 ton paddle wheels at 52rpm, achieving a service speed of 18 knots.

The sad remains of the *Royal Eagle* before she was scrapped.

The remains of the cocktail bar and boiler as the *Royal Eagle* slowly disappears. The *Royal Eagle* had been in service for little more than twenty years.

Two
Royal Daffodil

The magnificent *Royal Daffodil* built by Denny's of Dumbarton in 1939 became the favourite pleasure steamer of a generation of passengers and crew alike. *Royal Daffodil* spent the initial period after the cessation of hostilities in 1945 transporting army personnel stationed in Europe. She worked on both the Dover-Calais and Newhaven-Dieppe routes before entry into Thames service in 1947.

The *Royal Daffodil* undertaking trials on the Firth of Clyde prior to her maiden voyage to Calais on 28 April 1939. (Glasgow University Archives Service)

Scenes aboard the *Royal Daffodil*, c.1950. The *Royal Daffodil* offered a full silver service in the dining saloon for 118 passengers. A self-service cafeteria could accommodate a further 168 passengers. There were four bars as well as the soda fountain.

On departing from the first pier each morning, the *Royal Daffodil* always played the tune *Anchors Aweigh* over her loudspeaker system. At the end of the day's cruise Brahms *Cradle Song* serenaded passengers as they left the ship.

Capt. Paterson DSC served as Chief Officer to Capt. Johnson in the late 1930s on the paddle steamer *Thames Queen* and transferred to the new *Royal Daffodil* in 1939. He served on the *Royal Daffodil* throughout the hostilities along with Capt. Johnson. After the war, Capt. Paterson stayed with the *Royal Daffodil* until ill health forced him to transfer to the GSNC cargo ships in the late 1950s.

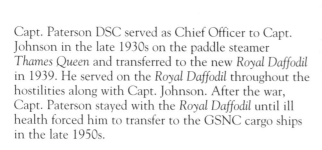

The *Royal Daffodil* was built as a one class vessel and carried a maximum of 2,073 on her Thames cruises. Modest pleasure steamers such as the *Royal Daffodil* carried on occasions half the number of passengers carried on the Atlantic 'Queens'. On the *Royal Daffodil* a crew of 113 ensured that these passengers enjoyed the cruise.

Royal Sovereign, *Queen of the Channel* and *Royal Daffodil* alongside Southend Pier, c.1960. A total of 5,158 passengers could be carried aboard these vessels at any one time!

Above:
Royal Daffodil alongside Margate Pier. Margate was always a popular destination. The Harbour Master and his deputy kept meticulous records of those disembarking to know how many might return later in the day. They also needed to collect the important pier dues of four pence per passenger.

"NO PASSPORT" DAY EXCURSIONS TO CALAIS AND BOULOGNE

M.V. "ROYAL DAFFODIL" from GRAVESEND and SOUTHEND piers

DETAILS of SAILINGS TIMES and FARES WITHIN

M.V. "QUEEN OF THE CHANNEL" from MARGATE, RAMSGATE & CLACTON

EAGLE STEAMERS
GENERAL STEAM NAVIGATION CO.
16 TRINITY SQUARE
LONDON, E.C.

Right:
Eagle Steamers brochure advertising Continental cruises, *c*.1960.

Programme

Tuesday, 30th May—**Arrival Day**

A reception desk will be in the booking hall at MARGATE British Railways (Southern Region) Station, where the British " Dunkirk Veterans " will be welcomed as they arrive and directed to their hosts' addresses. Badges will be worn so the guests may be identified.

9 p.m.   OFFICIAL WELCOME. His Worship the Mayor of Margate (Councillor C. B. Hosking) will welcome the " Dunkirk Veterans " in the Sun Lounge at the Winter Gardens. Music and Light Refreshments.

Wednesday, 31st May—**" The Daffodil " returns to Dunkirk**

11 a.m.   The " ROYAL DAFFODIL " will leave Margate Jetty for DUNKIRK. Members of the public wishing to make this special anniversary trip may obtain tickets (15/- for the return trip) at, the Jetty offices of the General Steam Navigation Company, on or before the day.

2 p.m.   The " ROYAL DAFFODIL " arrives at DUNKIRK. The Mayor of Margate goes ashore to be received by the Mayor of Dunkirk (M. Gustave Robelet). A Casket made of oak from the Holy Trinity Church, Margate (destroyed by enemy action in 1943) and containing sand from the Margate beach will be presented to the Mayor of Dunkirk.

3 p.m.   The Mayor of Dunkirk and the Mayor of Margate, with their parties, board the " ROYAL DAFFODIL ".

3.15 p.m.   The " ROYAL DAFFODIL " sails for MARGATE. Wreathes will be laid on the waters off the Dunkirk beaches.

6.30 p.m.   Arrival at MARGATE. Reception on the Jetty, with Guard of Honour provided by the Services.
> The Band of the Royal Marines School of Music, Deal.
> H.M.S. Bleasdale.
> 489 H.A.A. Regiment, Royal Artillery, T.A.
> 4/5th Battalion The Buffs, T.A.

The Mayor of Dunkirk will present a Casket of sand from the Dunkirk beaches.
The Parade, followed by the Mayoral parties and the " Dunkirk Veterans ", will proceed to the seafront entrance to the Winter Gardens, via the Lower Fort Promenade.

8.30 p.m. to 1 a.m.   CIVIC RECEPTION, BALL and CABARET at the Winter Gardens. British and Allied " Dunkirk Veterans ", and representatives of the Services and voluntary services at the time of the Evacuation of Dunkirk will be guests of His Worship the Mayor.
A limited number of tickets will be available to the public at 7/6 each, and can be obtained at the Information Bureau, Marine Terrace, and from the Winter Gardens.

PAGE FIFTY-THREE

On 31 May 1950, the *Royal Daffodil* returned to Dunkirk to commemorate the tenth anniversary of the evacuation. This is the programme from the souvenir brochure produced by Margate Town Council.

A photograph taken on the bridge of the *Royal Daffodil* during the Dunkirk anniversary cruise in 1950. Nearest to the camera is Capt. Johnson with Capt. Paterson in the centre. Both men had served on the *Royal Daffodil* during the Second World War and had many stories to tell of their experiences. They were both awarded the DSC for their service.

A postcard that must have been sent by thousands of visitors to Margate landing from an 'Eagle Steamer'. Apart from the fine beach, daytrippers might enjoy a visit to Dreamland with its forty acres of amusements, a dip in the Lido or a visit to the Shell Grotto.

Capt. Philip Kitto on the bridge of the *Royal Daffodil*, c.1955. Capt. Kitto spent his early career with the 'Queen Line' pleasure steamers on the River Medway, and became master of *Queen of Thanet* in the 1930s. After the war he was captain of the *Golden Eagle* until she was withdrawn in 1949. He later took over the command of the *Royal Daffodil*. He ran his ships in the naval tradition with good discipline and impeccable standards. Capt. Kitto died after a heart attack in the 1950s.

The familiar figure of Albert Robinson who was Berthing Master at Southend Pier from 1946-1959. He lived with his family in accommodation at the Pier Head and was kept very busy by the many vessels that used the pier at this time.

The *Royal Daffodil* and *Royal Sovereign* laid up in the West India Docks, London, during the winter period. The *Royal Daffodil* spent winter here whilst the *Royal Sovereign* sometimes wintered at the General Steam Navigation Company's Deptford Creek Wharf. The *Queen of the Channel* always spent the winter at Rochester.

Service aboard the pleasure steamers was always impeccable and stylish. These rare examples show the type of plated silverware found aboard the vessels. The teapot and sugar basin bear the General Steam Navigation Company crest, whilst the milk jug was used by the New Medway Steam Packet Company.

Taking afternoon tea in one of the spacious lounges was popular with many passengers.

PARTY MENUS for m.v. "Royal Daffodil" and m.v. "Royal Sovereign"

BREAKFAST
7/-d.

Cereal or Fruit Juice	Roll
Grilled Bacon and Fried Egg	Bread, Butter and Preserves
or	Tea or Coffee
Grilled Bacon and Sausage	

LUNCHEON

HOT

1. 7/-d.
Soup
Steak Pie
or
Steak Pudding
Fresh Peas, New Potatoes
Sweet or Biscuits, Butter, Cheese

2. 7/-d.
Soup
Lamb Chops
Fresh Peas, New Potatoes
Sweet or Biscuits, Butter, Cheese

3. 9/6d.
Soup
Poultry
Fresh Peas, New Potatoes
Sweet or Biscuits, Butter, Cheese

HOT or COLD

4. 7/6d.
Soup
Roast Beef
Fresh Peas, New Potatoes
Sweet or Biscuits, Butter, Cheese

COLD

5. 9/-d.
Dressed Crab Mayonnaise
Salad
Roll and Butter

6. 10/-d.
Fresh Salmon Mayonnaise
or
Half Lobster in Shell
Salad
Roll and Butter

HIGH TEA

1. 6/6d.
Fillet of Fish
French Fried Potatoes
Bread and Butter
Preserves
Tea

2. 7/-d.
Ham and Beef
Salad
Bread and Butter
Preserves
Tea

3. 9/6d.
Dressed Crab Mayonnaise
Salad
Bread and Butter
Preserves
Tea

4.—10/6d.
Salmon Mayonnaise
or
Half Lobster in Shell
Salad
Bread and Butter
Preserves
Tea

DINNER

12/6. From 6.30 p.m.
Soup
Fillet of Sole
Poultry
Baked and Boiled Potatoes : Fresh Peas
Sweet or Biscuits, butter and cheese

GRILLS 10/6
(10 minute order)
Fillet of Steak
French Fried Potatoes
Fresh Peas

MIXED GRILL 9/6
Lamb Chop
Bacon : Sausage
Liver : Tomato
French Fried Potatoes

Picnic Luncheon and Tea Cartons can be supplied, made up to Organiser's requirements. Prices on application.

This Tariff is subject to supplies being available on day of travel.

NOTE—Monday–Thursday : SPECIAL—FISH AND CHIPS : 5/-

Party menu for the *Royal Daffodil* and *Royal Sovereign* in 1964. Charters and party bookings provided much needed revenue during quiet parts of the season. By this time, catering costs were soaring and the General Steam Navigation Company had to heavily subsidise each meal by five shillings.

ROYAL DAFFODIL

Day Excursions

WITH PASSPORT - OR ONE
PASSPORT SIZE PHOTOGRAPH

From **GRAVESEND & SOUTHEND**

29th JUNE to 15th SEPTEMBER

To CALAIS | To BOULOGNE

SATURDAYS, SUNDAYS & MONDAYS | WEDNESDAYS

TIME TABLE

	OUT	HOME		OUT	HOME
GRAVESEND	dep. 8.45 a.m.	arr.10.15 p.m.	GRAVESEND	dep. 8.30 a.m.	arr. 10.15 p.m.
(West Pier, Stuart Road)		(approx.)	(West Pier, Stuart Road)		(approx.)
SOUTHEND	dep. 10.00 a.m.	arr. 9.00 p.m.	SOUTHEND	dep. 9.45 a.m.	arr. 9.00 p.m.
CALAIS ...	arr. 2.00 p.m.	dep. 5.00 p.m.	BOULOGNE	arr. 2.00 p.m.	dep. 5.00 p.m.
	(approx.)			(approx.)	

Fares for parties of 20
or more persons :
40/– adult ; 20/– child

DAY 45/- RETURN

Children under 3 years
free ; up to 14 years
half adult fare

BRITISH SUBJECTS ONLY : SEE NOTE 3 BACK PAGE

WEEKEND OR PERIOD RETURNS 60/– : SINGLE 37/6

Passports not essential for weekend passengers, i.e., out Sat./
Home Sun. or Mon—but passports are essential for longer
periods.   (Passports essential)

BICYCLES OR PRAMS : SINGLE 10/- : RETURN 20/-

FULLY LICENSED : EXCELLENT MEALS ON BOARD

COMBINED RAIL/BOAT THROUGH FARES

	Day Excursion	* Period or Weekend Returns		Day Excursion	* Period or Weekend Returns
Charing Cross/Waterloo	53/10	72/–	Woolwich Arsenal	50/8	67/6
London Bridge	53/–	71/–	Plumstead	50/8	67/6
New Cross	52/–	69/6	Abbey Wood	50/–	66/6
Lewisham	51/8	69/–	Dartford	48/–	63/6
Woolwich Dockyard	51/–	68/–	L'pool. St. & Fench. St. ...	54/–	—

* Calais only

The *Royal Daffodil's* programme for day excursions to Boulogne and Calais in 1964. On the long journey, passengers could hire a deckchair for 5s in the enclosed sun deck whilst listening to a commentary by means of loudspeakers, as well as hearing musical items and the BBC news at regular intervals.

The *Royal Daffodil* arrives back at Southend Pier on a charter in June 1955. The warship in the background is HMS *Glasgow*.

SOUTHEND PIER — LONGEST IN THE WORLD

Photograph by Hubert Thompson, A.R.P.S.

The *Royal Daffodil* departing from Southend Pier, *c*.1950 heading for Margate and then a cruise along the French coast. Unfortunately the *Royal Daffodil* was unable to call at French ports until the mid-1950s due to the wartime damage and government restrictions.

A deck scene aboard the *Royal Daffodil* on 30 May 1964. On the right is Harold Collard Stone who did a great deal to ensure that the heritage of Thames pleasure steamers survived.

"ROYAL DAFFODIL" LEAVING MARGATE PIER   L 929

The *Royal Daffodil* departing from Margate Pier.

Just visible on the funnels is the General Steam Navigation Company's houseflag. This was added after the Second World War. The letters were often a matter of debate amongst passengers and crew with humorous explanations such as 'God Save Nobbie Clark'.

A queue of passengers wait to join the *Royal Daffodil* at Southend, *c*.1955. Albert Robinson is carefully checking that everything is in order.

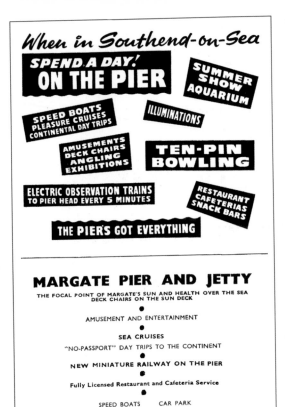

When passengers disembarked at either Southend or Margate they were confronted with an array of attractions on each pier. This page is from the official General Steam Navigation Company guide, c.1955.

In the late 1940s and early 1950s, packs of playing cards were sold aboard the pleasure steamers depicting vessels in the fleet.

EAGLE STEAMERS

in conjunction with CONTINENTAL COACH CHARTERING LTD

NOW INTRODUCE A NEW ECONOMY ROUTE TO

BARCELONA

from

GRAVESEND, TILBURY & SOUTHEND

Commencing MONDAY, 12th July until FRIDAY, 10th SEPTEMBER

£20-15-0 RETURN

TIMETABLE

OUT (Mondays only)				HOME (Fridays only)			
Gravesend	dep.	08.45 hrs. West Pier, Stuart Road		Barcelona	dep.	08.00 hrs. (Coach)	
Tilbury	,,	08.50 ,,		Toulouse	arr.	18.00 ,,	
Southend	,,	10.00 ,,		,,	dep.	21.30 ,, (Train)	
Calais	arr.	14.00 ,,	(Austerlitz Stn.)	Paris	arr.	06.15 ,, (Sat.)	
,,	dep.	14.30 ,, (Coach)		Paris	dep.	08.00 ,, (Coach)	
Paris	arr.	20.30 ,,		Calais	arr.	14.00 ,,	
Paris	dep.	22.45 ,, (Rail) (Austerlitz Stn.)		,,	dep.	17.00 ,,	
Toulouse	arr.	07.15 ,, (Tuesday)		Southend	arr.	21.00 ,,	
,,	dep.	09.30 ,, (Coach)		Tilbury	,,	22.00 ,,	
Barcelona	arr.	20.00 ,,		Gravesend	,,	22.15 ,,	

There will be a break for Lunch of One Hour on the outward journey between Toulouse and Barcelona, and on the homeward journey, between Barcelona and Toulouse. Lunch is NOT included in the fare

Fare does include reserved seat on train each way. Passengers requiring Couchette Sleeping Berths can obtain these through us (when available) at a cost of 25/- each way. Couchettes must be paid for on application. If unobtainable a full refund will be made. They are not transferable and no refund is allowed in the event of cancellation

Hotel Booking facilities are available at Hotel Rialto (21 days' notice required), Bed, Continental Breakfast and Lunch OR Dinner £1 10s. per day or £10 per week (Children £1 per day or £7 per week sharing parents' room)

PARTIES OF 20 OR MORE 10% REDUCTION

THIS NEW SERVICE OPERATES WITH THE OUTWARD JOURNEY COMMENCING ON MONDAYS AND THE HOMEWARD JOURNEY ON FRIDAYS

EAGLE STEAMERS
TOWER HILL, LONDON, E.C.3
Tel.: MINcing Lane 4451   OR AGENTS

Printed in Great Britain   B.H. Ltd. 3110/11/64

Few people would link the *Royal Daffodil* with the Costa Brava. However, in 1965 it was possible to travel by the *Royal Daffodil* from Gravesend, Tilbury and Southend to Calais where passengers joined a coach to Austerlitz station in Paris. There they were then put on a train to Toulouse before transferring to a coach taking them to Barcelona. Eagle Steamers even helped with booking accommodation. The journey took a total of twenty-two hours and may have been an experiment for the future?

The *Royal Daffodil* about to arrive at a pier, c.1955.

The *Royal Daffodil* navigates the Terneuzen-Ghent canal on her final slow journey to the breakers yard in February 1967 which the BBC recorded. She departed from the Thames amidst a mood of acceptance. Enthusiasts were still confident that the *Royal Sovereign* and *Queen of the Channel* might survive in some guise or other. *Royal Daffodil* was in excellent condition and had at least another forty years of service in front of her.

Three
Queen of the Channel

The *Queen of the Channel* at Deal Pier during the summer of 1964.

Lady Currie, wife of Sir William Currie who was Chairman of P&O, launched the *Queen of the Channel* on 25 February 1949. After the ceremony, Sir Maurice Denny who proposed the toast, 'The Ship, her Owners and her Godmother' presented Lady Currie with a momento of the occasion. *Queen of the Channel* left Denny's on 20 May and was finally delivered five days later. (Glasgow University Archives Service).

The number of the new *Queen of the Channel* was 1415, which compared with the first *Queen of the Channel*'s number of 1275. In just fourteen years, 140 ships had been built at the yard. Everybody was full of praise for the new ship. Capt. A. Hutton, Marine Superintendent of GSNC, remarked in his speech that 'The ship they had seen launched was a work of art'. (Glasgow University Archives Service).

The *Queen of the Channel* enters the Leven at the launch ceremony. Owing to the high tide in the Leven, the usual arrangements for the launch were varied. There was an interval of ninety minutes between the ceremony and lunch in the Model Hall. During this time the guests were split into three groups. One party went on a tour of Hiram Walker's Dumbarton Distillery, another toured a factory producing prefabricated houses whilst the last witnessed tests in the Leven Shipyard Experimental Tank. (Glasgow University Archives Service).

The forward dining saloon of the *Queen of the Channel, c.1960*.

The lounge and bar of the *Queen of the Channel, c.1960*.

Members of the Pier Head staff responsible for berthing the pleasure steamers at Southend, c.1950. Third from the left is Berthing Master, Albert Robinson.

Deal Pier was rebuilt following damage between 1954-1957 at a cost of £250,000 and was designed by Sir William Halcrow. *The Queen of the Channel* is seen here calling during a cross channel cruise, which were offered during the 1950s and 1960s from the pier.

The *Queen of the Channel* alongside Southend Pier, *c.*1960. The number of pleasure steamer calls to this well loved pier was in sharp decline at this time with only 134,973 passengers landed in 1961 against a figure of 278,655 in 1949.

The *Queen of the Channel* at Boulogne, *c.*1960.

The discharge certificate of James Toy, who was Second Engineer of the *Queen of the Channel* until the ship was withdrawn in 1966. Jim was lucky enough to be offered to take the *Queen of the Channel* to her new owners in Greece in 1966, but sadly had to decline the offer.

Dis. 1

CERTIFICATE OF DISCHARGE

FOR A SEAMAN DISCHARGED BEFORE A SUPERINTENDENT OR A CONSULAR OFFICER

Name of Ship and Official Number, Port of Registry and Gross Tonnage	Horse Power	Description of Voyage or Employment
M.V. QUEEN OF THE CHANNEL LONDON Off. No. 182023 G.T. 1471		H/T.

Name of Seaman	Date of Birth	Place of Birth
TOY. J.		Willington N.Z.

Rank or Rating	No. of R.N.R. Commission or Certif.	No. of Cert. (if any)
2/E.	—	—

Date of Engagement	Place of Engagement	Copy of Report of Character*	
		For Ability	For General Conduct
2.7.66.	Tilbury.		
Date of Discharge	Place of Discharge	VERY GOOD 57	
20.9.66.	Rochester.		

I certify *that the above particulars are correct and that the above named Seaman was discharged accordingly.*

Dated this .... day of 19

2 0 SEP 1966

.... MASTER.

AUTHENTICATED BY

.... Signature of Superintendent or Consular Officer.

* If the Seaman does not require a Certificate of his character, enter "Endorsement not required" in the spaces provided for the copy of the Report.

Signature of Seaman........................

NOTE.—Any person who forges or fraudulently alters any Certificate or Report, or copy of a Report, or who makes use of any Certificate or Report, or copy of a Report, which is forged or altered or does not belong to him, shall for each such offence be deemed guilty of a misdemeanor, and may be fined or imprisoned.

N.B.—Should this Certificate come into the possession of any person to whom it does not belong, it should be handed to the Superintendent of the nearest Mercantile Marine Office, or be transmitted to the Registrar-General of Shipping and Seamen, Cardiff.

(S.18961) Wt.64668/M2926 300 Bks. 3/62 Hw.-TA-78

The *Queen of the Channel* at Calais. In 1964 the cost of a day return was £2 from Margate, Ramsgate or Deal and gave up to five hours ashore in France.

11/- Tour to CAP BLANC NEZ

(about 1 hr. 30 mins.).

("ROYAL DAFFODIL" and "QUEEN OF THE CHANNEL")

Departure from " Quai de la Colonne " (coaches waiting alongside ship) — Calais beach and sea front — Bleriot-Plage (Bleriot Memorial) — Sangate (formerly Sandgate)—Site of work on ventilation shaft for the Channel Tunnel — Site of German bunkers and gun sites 1940/45—Latham Memorial (panoramic views of surrounding countryside)—Cap Blanc-Nez (views of the Channel, North Sea and Cliffs of Dover)—Wissant (formerly White Sands)—Stop for refreshments (not included)—St. Inglevert (Canadian War Cemetery 1945)—Calais—Disembark near Town Hall with time for shopping before returning to ship.

14/- Tour to CAP GRIS NEZ

(about 2 hrs.).

("QUEEN OF THE CHANNEL" from Thanet only)

Departure from " Quai de la Colonne " (coaches alongside ship)—through the town of Calais to Guines (occupied by British troops for 200 years) — Guines Forest — Fiennes — Marquise — Vallee Heureuse — (Happy Valley) — Cap Gris Nez (starting point for cross-channel swimmers) — Wissant (formerly White Sands)—Stop for refreshments (not included) — Cap Blanc-Nez (views of the Channel, North Sea and Cliffs of Dover)—Latham Memorial (panoramic views of surrounding countryside)—Site of German bunkers and gun sites 1940/45—Site of work on ventilation shaft for the Channel Tunnel—Sangate (formerly Sandgate) — Bleriot-Plage (Bleriot Memorial)—Calais beach and sea front—Disembark near Town Hall with time for shopping before returning to ship.

24/- LUNCH at WISSANT

("QUEEN OF THE CHANNEL" from Thanet only).

Departure from " Quai de la Colonne " (coaches waiting alongside the ship)—Calais beach and sea front — Bleriot-Plage (Bleriot Memorial) — Sangate (formerly Sandgate)—Site of work of ventilation shaft for the Channel Tunnel — Site of German bunkers and guns 1940/45 — Latham Memorial (panoramic views of the Channel) — Cap Blanc Nez (views of the Channel, North Sea and Cliffs of Dover) — Wissant (formerly White Sands)—Continental Lunch at restaurant situated in view of the Channel—Approximately one hour free time—Return to Calais by the same way—Disembarking near Town Hall with time for shopping before returning to ship (about 25 minutes walk from Town Hall).

A popular feature aboard *Queen of the Channel* and *Royal Daffodil* were the combined coach and bus tours of French coastal attractions. By the mid-1950s, the wartime beaches and gun emplacements had become attractions for daytrippers to visit. For a surcharge of 14s, these attractions could be visited along with an opportunity for shopping in Calais and lunch before rejoining *Queen of the Channel* for the trip back home.

Queen of the Channel photographed from the *Medway Queen* in June 1955.

Second Engineer, James Toy (right) with a colleague standing next to the galley aboard the *Queen of the Channel*.

M.V. "QUEEN OF THE CHANNEL" 1964 SAILINGS

JUNE

		From	a.m.			a.m.	To
Sat.	6th June	Margate	9.45	Deal	11.00		Boulogne
Sun.	7th ,,	Ramsgate	10.00	Deal	11.00		Boulogne
Tues.	9th ,,	Ramsgate	10.00	Deal	11.00		Calais
Wed.	10th ,,	Margate	10.00	Deal	11.15		Boulogne
Tues.	16th ,,	Ramsgate	10.00	Deal	10.50		Dunkirk
Wed.	17th ,,	Margate	10.00	Deal	11.15		Boulogne
Sat.	20th ,,	Margate	9.45	Deal	11.00		Calais
Sun.	21st ,,	Ramsgate	10.00	Deal	10.50		Dunkirk
Tues.	23rd ,,	Ramsgate	10.00	Deal	11.00		Boulogne
Wed.	24th ,,	Margate	10.00	Deal	11.15		Calais
Sat.	27th ,,	Margate	9.45	Deal	11.00		Boulogne
Sun.	28th ,,	Ramsgate	10.00	Deal	11.00		Calais
Tues.	30th ,,	Ramsgate	10.00	Deal	11.00		Boulogne

JULY

		From	a.m.			a.m.	To
Wed.	1st July	Margate	10.00	Deal	11.15		Calais
Sat.	4th ,,	Margate	9.40	Deal	10.50		Dunkirk
Sun.	5th ,,	Ramsgate	10.00	Deal	11.00		Boulogne
Tues.	7th ,,	Ramsgate	10.00	Deal	11.00		Boulogne
Wed.	8th ,,	Margate	10.00	Deal	11.15		Calais
Sat.	11th ,,	Margate	9.45	Deal	11.00		Boulogne
Sun.	12th ,,	Margate	10.00	Deal	11.15		Calais
Mon.	13th ,,	Ramsgate	10.00	Deal	11.00		Calais
Tues.	14th ,,	Margate	10.00				Boulogne
Wed.	15th ,,	Margate	10.45				Calais
Fri.	17th ,,	Ramsgate	10.00	Deal	11.00		Boulogne
Sun.	19th ,,	Ramsgate	10.00	Deal	11.00		Boulogne
Mon.	20th ,,	Ramsgate	10.00	Deal	10.50		Dunkirk
Tues.	21st ,,	Margate	10.00				Boulogne
Wed.	22nd ,,	Margate	10.45				Calais
Fri.	24th ,,	Ramsgate	10.00	Deal	11.00		Boulogne
Sun.	26th ,,	Margate	9.40	Deal	10.50		Dunkirk
Mon.	27th ,,	Ramsgate	10.00	Deal	11.00		Calais
Tues.	28th ,,	Margate	10.00				Boulogne
Wed.	29th ,,	Margate	10.45				Calais
Fri.	31st ,,	Ramsgate	10.00	Deal	11.00		Boulogne

AUGUST

		From	a.m.			a.m.	To
Sun.	2nd August	Ramsgate	10.00	Deal	11.00		Boulogne
Mon.	3rd ,,	Ramsgate	10.00	Deal	10.50		Dunkirk
Tues.	4th ,,	Margate	10.00				Boulogne
Wed.	5th ,,	Margate	10.45				Calais
Fri.	7th ,,	Ramsgate	10.00	Deal	11.00		Boulogne
Sun.	9th ,,	Margate	10.00	Deal	11.15		Boulogne
Mon.	10th ,,	Ramsgate	10.00	Deal	11.00		Calais
Tues.	11th ,,	Margate	10.00				Boulogne
Wed.	12th ,,	Margate	10.15				Dunkirk
Fri.	14th ,,	Ramsgate	10.00	Deal	11.00		Boulogne
Sun.	16th ,,	Ramsgate	10.00	Deal	11.00		Calais
Tues.	18th ,,	Margate	10.00	Deal	11.15		Boulogne
Wed.	19th ,,	Margate	10.00	Deal	11.15		Calais
Fri.	21st ,,	Ramsgate	10.00	Deal	10.50		Dunkirk
Sat.	22nd ,,	Ramsgate	10.00	Deal	11.00		Boulogne
Sun.	23rd ,,	Margate	9.40	Deal	10.50		Dunkirk
Mon.	24th ,,	Ramsgate	10.00	Deal	11.00		Calais
Tues.	25th ,,	Margate	10.00	Deal	11.15		Boulogne
Wed.	26th ,,	Margate	10.45				Calais

SEPTEMBER

		From	a.m.			a.m.	To
Tues.	1st Sept.	Ramsgate	10.00	Deal	11.00		Boulogne
Wed.	2nd ,,	Margate	10.00	Deal	11.15		Calais
Sat.	5th ,,	Ramsgate	10.00	Deal	10.50		Dunkirk
Sun.	6th ,,	Margate	10.00	Deal	11.15		Calais
Tues.	8th ,,	Ramsgate	10.00	Deal	11.00		Boulogne
Wed.	9th ,,	Margate	10.00	Deal	11.15		Calais
Sat.	12th ,,	Margate	9.45	Deal	11.00		Calais
Sun.	13th ,,	Ramsgate	10.00	Deal	10.45		Boulogne

In 1964 *Queen of the Channel* undertook an ambitious programme of cruises from the Kent Coast to Boulogne, Calais and Dunkirk. By the late 1950s the number of passengers on the 'non passport' trips was in decline, but still in 1960, 78,031 people enjoyed a cruise along the French coast.

James Toy relaxing during a rare moment off duty with his son Robin. Robin often spent his summer holiday with his father aboard the *Queen of the Channel*.

The *Queen of the Channel* at Clacton during the 1949 season.

Queen of the Channel leaving London, c.1965. You can clearly see the dockside cranes that have since disappeared.

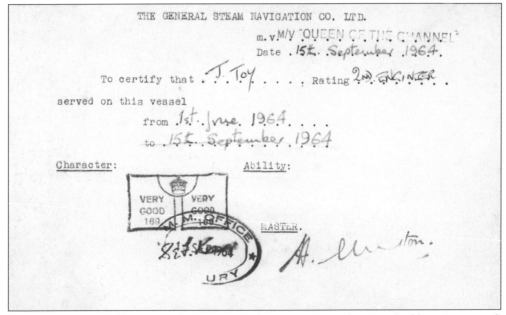

THE GENERAL STEAM NAVIGATION CO. LTD.

m. v. M/V "QUEEN OF THE CHANNEL"

Date .15th. September .1964.

To certify that .J. Toy. . . . , Rating 2nd. ENGINEER . .

served on this vessel

from .1st. June. 1964. . . .

to .15th. September. 1964

Character: Ability:

VERY GOOD 189   VERY GOOD 189

MASTER.

The certificate signed by Capt. Clayton stating that James Toy's character had been 'very good' during the 1964 season.

The cover of the 'Eagle Steamers' guide *What's What in Shipping*, was sold aboard the vessels in the 1950s and 1960s. It included an illustrated guide to points of interest along the route as well as maritime information that might be useful to passengers.

Queen of the Channel entering the harbour at Boulogne, c.1964.

The end of an era as the *Queen of the Channel* departs from Ramsgate for the very last time in 1966.

The *Queen of the Channel* was sold in 1968 for further service as *Oia* in the Greek Islands. She was re-named as *Leto* in 1976 before finally being scrapped at Eleusis in 1984.

Four
Royal Sovereign

The *Royal Sovereign* photographed on trials on the Firth of Clyde, 15 July 1948. She achieved a trials speed of 20.5 knots.

Royal Sovereign was launched on 7 May 1948 by Mrs Lang, wife of one of the directors of the General Steam Navigation Company. After the ceremony, Sir Maurice Denny presented her with a diamond brooch as a momento of the occasion before proposing the toast, 'The Ship, her Godmother and the Owners'. (Glasgow University Archives Service).

A historic moment as the *Royal Sovereign* enters the water for the first time. Denny's were prolific builders of 'quality' ships and, in 1947 alone, twenty ships were in the process of being built. In the reply to Sir Maurice Denny's speech, Mr R. Kelso (Chairman GSNC) reflected on the quality of the ships built for the company by Denny's. (Glasgow University Archives Service).

This historic photograph shows the launch party gathered for the formal photograph. (Glasgow University Archives Service)

The first TSMV *Royal Sovereign* was launched in April 1937 and with her stablemate *Queen of the Channel*, signalled a revolution in Thames excursion steamer design. She was the first to have side 'blisters', measuring 150ft in length, which greatly extended the passenger accommodation and acted as stabilisers to reduce rolling, but her career was brief; in 1940 she was sunk by a mine in the Bristol Channel. The new *Royal Sovereign* replaced the vessel in 1948.

The *Royal Sovereign* departing from London on one of her regular cruises to Southend and Margate, *c.*1951. In the following year, an additional stop was made at North Woolwich Pier to embark and disembark passengers.

M.V. ROYAL SOVEREIGN
Sun Deck

The sun deck of the *Royal Sovereign*. The ship is alongside Tower Pier with part of the GSNC flag emblem visible on the funnel. The spacious decks can be appreciated in this photograph. She had an overall length of 288ft.

The main dining saloon of the *Royal Sovereign*, c.1955.

Lounge deck and cocktail bar of the *Royal Sovereign*, c.1955.

The smoke room of the *Royal Sovereign*, c.1955.

An entrance lounge of the *Royal Sovereign*, c.1955.

The *Royal Sovereign*'s main engines. The *Royal Sovereign* was powered by two twelve-cylinder, two-stroke Sulzer diesel engines. With the ship only running for a short season each year, the engines were always kept in good condition. The General Steam Navigation Company took great pride in the high standards of presentation in these areas.

The forward dining saloon of the *Royal Sovereign*, *c*.1955.

The *Royal Sovereign* departing from London.

The *Royal Sovereign* photographed on 17 June 1965 towards the end of her Thames career.

Royal Sovereign departing from Margate Pier. Short sea cruises from Margate were very popular. In 1949 a short cruise to see the Tongue Fort cost 4s.

Passengers embarking on the *Royal Sovereign* at North Woolwich Pier, *c*.1955.

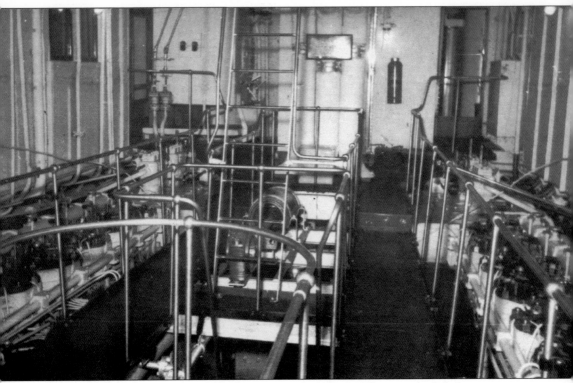

The upper engine room on the *Royal Sovereign*. Note the windows on the left for passengers to see the tops of the 12-cylinder, Sulzer two-stroke engines.

M.V. "ROYAL SOVEREIGN"

THE POPULAR LONDON MOTOR VESSEL

"Royal Sovereign" arrives in Margate

TODAY (and every day except Fridays)

(Also excepting 18th August)

At 2.40 p.m. she leaves on her Pleasant 15 Miles Coastal Cruise towards Kingsgate, North Foreland, Broadstairs, etc.

Returning by 3.45 p.m.

On TUESDAYS ONLY the Cruise is around The Tongue Fort, the Estuary Anti-Aircraft Defences of the Last War.

5/- Return (CHILDREN UNDER 14 YEARS HALF CHILDREN UNDER 3 FREE)

From the JETTY, MARGATE, 2.40 p.m.

Handbill detailing the short cruises undertaken by the *Royal Sovereign* from Margate.

A picture postcard *c.*1960 depicting the spacious and luxurious accommodation of the *Royal Sovereign*. These vessels were called 'London's Luxury Liners'.

The *Royal Sovereign* departing from Margate Pier. The pier had been designed by the famous Victorian engineer Eugenius Birch and survived until 1978 when it was wrecked by a storm.

The *Royal Sovereign* photographed from the *Medway Queen* in June 1955, whilst on charter to D. Rose & Sons for their cruise to Clacton.

Catering aboard the pleasure steamers was always of a high standard.

A rare photograph taken aboard the *Royal Sovereign* of James Toy, Third Engineer (left) along with two colleagues.

A rare moment of relaxation as officers are joined by their families and friends on the bridge of the *Royal Sovereign*. It was taken on one of her off service days during the 1950s in the Pool of London.

Engineering crew at the engine room controls of the *Royal Sovereign*.

The livery of the motor vessels was very distinctive with a white hull, light olive green boot topping and a buff funnel. A badge on the stem was painted in appropriate heraldic colours. *Royal Sovereign* carried six 27ft lifeboats, of which one was motorised.

SCENIC VIEW
Cocktail
COASTER

CUT ON DOTTED LINE

Souvenirs took many shapes and forms aboard the pleasure steamers. This colour postcard dating from the 1960s could, with a pair of scissors, be transformed into an attractive 'cocktail coaster'.

Royal Sovereign leaving London with the *Royal Eagle* at Tower Pier. On the right of the picture are the Irongate and St Katherines Wharves owned by the GSNC. The site is now occupied by the Tower Hotel.

Royal Sovereign passing Gravesend. Many men from the town served aboard the General Steam Navigation Company vessels. For many years the familiar figure of Mr H.F. Loft acted as Port Agent until the demise of the ships in 1966. His family had acted in this capacity for more than seventy years from premises in New Road.

The *Royal Sovereign* arriving at Margate Pier during her first season in 1948. She had sailed on her maiden voyage from London to Margate and Ramsgate.

Officers enjoying lunch in the dining saloon of the *Royal Sovereign*, c.1960. Third Engineer, James Toy, is seated on the left.

James Toy and fellow crewmen from the engine room of the *Royal Sovereign* enjoying a few moments of relaxation away from the heat and noise of their workplace. Working life in such conditions must have been uncomfortable during the summer months and there was little Health & Safety protection.

The main fuse panel of the *Royal Sovereign*.

Handbill advertising cruises to Margate from Southend aboard the *Royal Sovereign* in 1963. Such cruises were aimed at the holidaymaker who had plenty of time after breakfast to make their way to the pier head before joining the ship for Margate. After time ashore, they still arrived back in time for dinner or to see a show.

From 1st **JUNE** until **15th SEPT. 1963**
DAILY (except . Fridays)
No Sailings on Sunday. 16th June & Sunday, 18th August

THE TWIN-SCREW M.V.

"ROYAL SOVEREIGN"

will sail from SOUTHEND PIER

at **12.0** noon

allowing up to TWO HOURS ashore at

MARGATE

The popular Holiday Resort on the Kent coast

SINGLE		PERIOD RETURN
12/-	Day **15/-** Return	20/-

Children under 14 years Half fare; under 3 years, Free
Tickets Booked at the Pier Hill Office (Shore End) include Admission to the Pier

TIMES

Due Margate at 2.0 p.m.　　　　Depart Margate at 4.0 p.m.
Back at Southend 6.0 p.m. approx.

Fully Licensed　:　Restaurant Service　:　Light Refreshments
SPECIAL RATES FOR PARTIES BOOKED IN ADVANCE

Sailings are subject to weather and other circumstances permitting
FOR CONDITIONS OF CARRIAGE SEE OVERLEAF

EAGLE STEAMERS

PIER HILL, SOUTHEND-ON-SEA. Telephone: 68597 (May/Sept.)

(P.T.O

Southend Pier *c*.1965 shows the Eagle & Queen Line Steamers booking office. Prospective passengers can be seen looking at the departure boards for the week which offered a wide array of cruises.

Eagle Steamers poster advertising cruises to Calais and Boulogne in 1964.

DAY EXCURSIONS by M/v ROYAL SOVEREIGN
from GREAT YARMOUTH - FISHWHARF (No. 4 SHED)

to CALAIS & DUNKIRK

Every Sunday & Wednesday to CALAIS
Every Tuesday to DUNKIRK
(NO SAILING ON TUESDAY 31st MAY)

Commencing Sun. 29th May to Sunday 11th Sept.

	OUT		HOME
GT. YARMOUTH	dep. 0830 hrs.	CALAIS or DUNKIRK dep. 1700 hrs.	
CALAIS or DUNKIRK arr. 1430 hrs. appx.		GT. YARMOUTH	arr. 2300 hrs.

DAY 52/- RETURN

A reduced rate of **45/-** for prebooked parties of 20 or more. Children under 3 years free - up to 16 years half fare.

DAY EXCURSIONS ARE WITH PASSPORT OR ONE FULL FACED PASSPORT SIZE PHOTOGRAPH BRITISH SUBJECTS ONLY (See Note 2 Back Page)

Passengers must be at FISHWHARF half an hour before sailing time for Customs and Immigration formalities.

Wines and Spirits for consumption on board at duty free prices.

to CLACTON approx 3 hours Ashore

Every Monday at 0930 hrs. Commencing 6th June

	OUT		HOME
GT. YARMOUTH dep. 0930 hrs.		CLACTON	dep. 1630 hrs.
CLACTON	arr. 1330 hrs. appx.	GT. YARMOUTH arr. 2030 hrs.	

DAY 25/- RETURN

Passengers wishing to remain on board for the afternoon Sea Trip may do so on payment of **5/-**

also A GRAND 7 hr. SEACRUISE
TO VIEW THE OIL RIGS

Every Friday, Commencing Friday, 3rd June
SAILING at 1030 hrs. RETURNING 1730 hrs.

ROUND 25/- TRIP

On both these services there is a reduced rate for prebooked parties of 30 or over of **22/6.**
Children under 3 years free - up to 16 years half fare

FULLY LICENSED BARS ON BOARD

A special fare will be quoted for all services to organised parties of old age pensioners and various charitable organisations, provided they are travelling early or late season, on a midweek day.

CATERING FACILITIES — LIGHT REFRESHMENTS — AMUSEMENTS

Passengers are advised that when tides are unfavourable the times of arrival may be somewhat later than shown in the timetable. All sailings are subject to alteration without notice and to weather and other circumstances permitting.

Details of day excursions by *Royal Sovereign* from Great Yarmouth in 1966. A grand seven hour sea cruise was offered to see the oil rigs for 25s or for 52s, you could visit Calais or Dunkirk.

GSN

EAGLE STEAMERS

SAILING FROM
THE FISH WHARF
GREAT YARMOUTH

BY
M/V ROYAL SOVEREIGN
**TO CALAIS
DUNKIRK
CLACTON &-
NORTH SEA OIL RIGS**

(See Back Page for Conditions of Carriage and Important Notes)

Book at:
G.S.N.
EAGLE STEAMERS
24 FISHWHARF (No. 4 Shed)
GREAT YARMOUTH
NORFOLK

Manager for Gt. Yarmouth
W. A. BROOKS

Telephone: GT. YARMOUTH 55192 and 55379   OR AGENTS

By 1966 the writing was on the wall as the *Royal Sovereign* was placed for the first time in her career on the cross channel service to Dunkirk and Calais out of Great Yarmouth. The General Steam Navigation Company in their announcement on 20 December 1966, claimed that losses had reached £170,000 in the past year alone. The long tradition of taking an 'Eagle Steamer' trip to the sea from London was at an end. *Royal Sovereign* was purchased by Townsend Ferries in April 1966. She initially became a ferry between Dover and Zeebrugge under the name of *Autocarrier*.

The stern of *Royal Sovereign*, now named *Ischia*, on 9 September 2000. She now provides a ferry service from Pozzuoli near Naples, to the port of Casamicciola on the island of Ischia.

Isola di San Martino and Monte di Procida seen from the foredeck of *Ischia* on 11 September 2000.

Ischia is now the last survivor of the three famous General Steam Navigation Company motor vessels. This photograph shows the many changes to the ship in the thirty-four years since she left the Thames but if you look closely, you can still make out some features of *Royal Sovereign*.

The *Royal Sovereign* in her Thames heyday.

Five

Other Vessels

The *Medway Queen* departing from Southend on 31 August 1963.

THE "ROYAL EAGLE" AND THE "QUEEN OF THANET" AT MARGATE.

9064.

The *Queen of Thanet* and *Royal Eagle* at Margate Pier. Originally an ex-Ascot class minesweeper of the First World War, *Queen of Thanet* did sterling work during the Second World War and re-entered service on the Thames in 1946.

The *Queen of Kent* at Ramsgate in August 1947. Purchased by the New Medway Steam Packet Company in 1927, this ex-minesweeper was converted as a pleasure steamer and worked on the Medway and Thames. With the introduction of the *Royal Sovereign* and *Queen of the Channel* after the war, this vessel was surplus to requirements and was sold along with *Queen of Thanet* to Red Funnel Steamers of Southampton for further service in December 1948.

Medway Queen was built in 1924 by Ailsa of Troon. Initially she ran between Rochester and Southend but later served Herne Bay and Clacton. Here she is seen arriving back at Southend Pier after a cruise to the Kent Coast.

The *Medway Queen* lying alongside Herne Bay Pier.

D. ROSE, LTD.

SOUVENIR BROCHURE
OF A SPECIAL CRUISE TO
CLACTON ON JUNE 16TH, 1955
BY
P.S. "MEDWAY QUEEN"

The souvenir brochure printed for a special charter arranged by Don Rose on 16 June 1955. It was arranged as a thank you for customer's loyalty during the upheaval of the Second World War. The charter was heralded as perhaps 'the very last occasion when a paddle steamer of any kind chugged its way down from the Tower to the sea'.

Medway Queen leaving the Upper Pool of London on her non-stop charter to Clacton for Don Rose. It was a glorious day and a great success providing another reason for Don to later think of running a paddle steamer service on the Thames.

Marjorie Fuller standing alongside Charlie, the well known Purser of the *Medway Queen*, *c*.1955. Charlie was a great lover of music and often played classical music including the Proms, over the ship's loudspeaker system.

Medway Queen carried up to 828 people on the Southend run and once had a certificate for 980 for Sheerness. Her record for maintaining a service was unequalled and the company would often run the ship with only twenty passengers aboard.

Sheerness Pier had been a regular calling point for *Medway Queen* until its closure in 1954. This photograph was taken in 1949.

A stunning photograph of *Medway Queen* taken *c.*1960 that captures the atmosphere of a traditional Thames paddle steamer.

Medway Queen had an open bridge until the end of her career in 1963. Capt. Leonard Horsham is seen here on a fine day in 1963. Capt. Horsham was master of the vessel from the end of the war until she finished in 1963. During the last few weeks of service, when TV reporters and journalists swarmed aboard the ship, Capt. Horsham became quite weary of the intense media attention. In pure Churchillian fashion, Leonard Horsham let vent with the words 'Never has a ship been photographed so much by so many'.

Medway Queen was withdrawn on 8 September 1963 after farewell speeches at the piers that she had served for thirty-nine years. Business had dwindled in the years prior to withdrawal but the cost of the annual survey (£4,000) was also a consideration. The Paddle Steamer Preservation Society did their best to save her and eventually she was sold to a catering firm of the Forte group who planned to moor her on the Thames off Dolphin Square. This venture fell through and she was then sold to Ridett's on the Isle of Wight to become the Medway Queen Club. After many years of neglect she returned to the Medway in 1984.

Medway Queen has now spent as much time in preservation as she spent in operation. The dedicated work of the Medway Queen Preservation Society has ensured her survival but her condition is fragile. *Medway Queen* is the last remaining Thames paddle steamer.

In 1947, the New Medway Steam Packet Company purchased a small vessel to run a service between Sheerness and Herne Bay. *Rochester Queen* entered service in 1948 and could carry up to 425 passengers. She provided a variety of cruises, including some from Clacton, before being sold to German owners in 1956.

UNTIL FURTHER NOTICE –

GRAND CRUISES • • By the Twin-Screw Turbine Steamer

"LADY ENCHANTRESS"

THE FIRST-CLASS PULLMAN COMFORT STEAMER

LEAVING SOUTHEND PIER AT 9.30 a.m.

DAILY (Fridays Excepted)

MARGATE 7'6 Return

ABOUT 5½ HOURS ASHORE [UNDER 14 HALF FARE]

EXCELLENT CATERING • ALL KINDS OF REFRESHMENTS
FULLY LICENCED

No Extra Charge for Sun Deck

No Extra Fares to Pay for Saturdays or Sundays

Sundays, Tuesdays Thursdays & Saturdays		Mondays and Wednesdays
To within a short distance of the **Famous Dunkirk-Calais Beaches**	**Special Full Day Cruises**	**THE CRUISE TO MARGATE** About 2 hours at Margate and a Grand Cruise for Remainder of Day
Return Fares: From Southend **15/-** Under 14 Half-fare	All Sailings, etc., Weather and Other Circumstances Permitting	Return Fares: From Southend **14/-** Under 14 Half-fare

DUE BACK AT SOUTHEND 7.40 p.m.

BOOK AT THE THREE STAR LINE

PIER HILL and PIER HEAD, SOUTHEND

Passengers are carried only on the terms and conditions printed on the Company's tickets

THE THREE STAR LINE, Southend Office, Marine 67945. Head Office, Ramsgate 1212

Printed by W. H. Houlderson, Ltd., 49-55, London Road, Southend-on-Sea.

Lady Enchantress entered service on the Thames in 1947. She had been purchased for £22,500 by three theatrical people and was converted at a staggering cost of £190,000. She ran from Gravesend to Southend and Margate as well as a number of other cruises. She carried a total of 46,860 passengers on just thirty-three trips, which indicates her popularity. Unfortunately, the high cost of the conversion and the shortness of the season meant that she was withdrawn from service and never again operated on the Thames.

Anzio I taken from the stern of the *Medway Queen, c.*1963, whilst alongside at Southend Pier. *Anzio I* remained in service until the end of that year and, after a period of lay-up at Tilbury, was sold for further service at Inverness. She sailed on 1 April 1966, but was hit by a terrible storm off Spurn Head and was totally wrecked with the loss of her entire crew.

Anzio I was built in 1908 as *Lochinvar*. She had a Class 4 certificate for 351 passengers and provided service on the Sheerness ferry from Southend. This photograph clearly shows the crane that was a remnant of her career with the MacBrayne fleet in Scotland.

The *Londoner* appeared on the Thames in July 1965. Originally named the *Stena Nordica*, this ship ran a daily return service between Tilbury and Calais. This ferry service allowed passengers the novel opportunity of sampling a Scandinavian style *smorgasbord* and bingo. Sadly, the British public enjoyed this new experience to such an extent that the service resulted in a severe loss of passengers to the General Steam Navigation Company, with whose services it competed. Despite the introduction of extra vessels, the service was stopped in 1968, but it was too late for the GSNC vessels.

COMMENCING MAY 19th for the 1962 SEASON

H 222

M.V. ANZIO I
Daily Service
Southend-on-Sea - Sheerness

FULLY LICENSED BAR, TEAS & REFRESHMENTS ON BOARD

Luxurious Lounges and Observation Saloon

FRIDAYS EXCEPTED

Except Friday, August 3rd and 10th when vessel will run.
No Sailing Wednesday, 27th June

Boat leaves Southend Pier Head	6 UP TO HOURS ON THE LOVELY ISLE OF SHEPPEY KENT'S HOLIDAY ISLE	Bus leaves Sheerness Coach Station
11.15 a'm.		10.00 a.m.
*2.45 p.m.		12.00 noon
5.00 p.m.		3.30 p.m.
7.00 p.m.		5.45 p.m.

(11.15 a.m. every Wednesday—Canterbury staying 3 hrs. 12s. return)
(COMBINED BOAT & COACH TRIP)

Passengers not wishing to land, may have round trip of 1½ hours
Landing Passengers may return at any of the above times

*The 2.45 p.m. journey includes a special estuary cruise. Arriving back at Southend at 4.30 p.m. Fare 4s.

BOAT FARES

Landing Return	......	......	7/-
Single...	.....	......	5/-
Non-Landing Return		......	4/-

CHILDREN HALF PRICE

Buses meet every boat for Coach Station, from whence frequent services are operated to all parts of the Island, including Leysdown and Minster.

All Passengers landing at Sheerness must travel through Harbour Estate by Bus to and from Coach Station. Fare 3d.

THAMES & MEDWAY NAVIGATION COMPANY LTD

BOOKING OFFICES:
SOUTHEND PIER HEAD — OR PIER ENTRANCE
Phone: 63027

REDUCED RATES FOR PRIVATE PARTIES
AVAILABLE FOR CHARTER EVENINGS & FRIDAYS

(Weather and other circumstances permitting)

THE APOLLO PRESS (Southend) LTD., 444 Southchurch Road, Southend-on-Sea.

Handbill for *Anzio I* for the 1962 season. Passengers were able to take a short cruise to the Isle of Sheppey or could combine the cruise with a coach trip to Canterbury, Maidstone or Herne Bay on payment of a small supplement.

Another paddle steamer on the Thames

BUT ONLY FO A WEEK

THE Medway Queen will not now be the last paddle steamer to ply from Southend Pier. On Sunday the Consul (below) will tie up at the Pier and for a week will provide pleasure trips on the Thames.

ne Consul is the oldest vessel of its type in regular service in the British Isles. Built in 1896 by R. and H. Green, of Blackwall, it was originally in service in the Torquay area.

hen she returns to the Thames next week it will be the first time her paddles have churned these waters since she was launched 67 years ago. Originally known as the Duke of Devonshire, she has a gross tonnage of 277, is 175 feet long, 20 feet wide and capable of developing 100 horse power.

rlier this year she was completely overhauled and modernised. Her accommodation now includes a dining saloon, novelty shop, soda fountain and two bars. The atmosphere of antiquity has been preserved in one of the saloons, which has been fitted out as "The Fisherman's Retreat."

Paddle steamer Consul

In 1963, the Victorian paddle steamer *Consul* returned to the Thames where she had been built in 1896. She had spent her career on the south coast but in 1963 had been chartered by New Belle Steamers, inspired by Don Rose, and ran cruises from 15 to 22 September. This venture was very much a try-out for the more ambitious introduction of the *Queen of the South* by Don Rose in 1966-1967.

The *Consul* at Southend Pier on her last day of Thames service, 22 September 1963. On that day it was possible to cruise to Southend for time ashore or to stay aboard for a cruise across to the River Medway.

Consul alongside Southend Pier. She is about to depart for a cruise to Herne Bay.

NEW BELLE STEAMERS
ANNOUNCE A SERIES OF SPECIAL SEPTEMBER
Sea Cruises from Southend
BY THE FAMOUS PADDLE STEAMER 'CONSUL'
Meals & Refreshments served in comfortable saloons at very reasonable prices. Music on Board
FULLY LICENCED BAR OPEN ALL DAY

Tuesday **17th** September	**AT 12.15pm.** Arr. Back App. 6.30 pm	**Day return to HERNE BAY** Allowing over 2 hours ashore. Passengers may also remain on board for special cruise from Herne Bay.	Day Return **ONLY 9/6** Inc: Sea Cruise **14/-**
	AT 6.30 pm.	**Single trip to GRAVESEND** Ample time to return by train & ferry to Southend.	Single Fare **4/6**
Wednesday **18th** September	**3.45pm.** Returning At App: 5.10pm.	**Delightful Afternoon Sea Cruise** To view the River Medway, Kentish Coast, Isles of Grain & Sheppey.	REDUCED Return Fare **4/-**
	AT 5.15pm. Arriving Back About 9.00pm	**Musical SHOWBOAT Cruise** Special Evening Up River to **Gravesend and Tilbury** A wonderful opportunity to view the Illuminations. **BAND ON BOARD NON LANDING**	Return Fare **8/6**
Thursday **19th** September	**AT 2.35pm** Returning 4.15pm.	**Afternoon Sea Cruise** To view the Essex Coast, passing Shoeberryness Foulness & the Maplin Sands.	MIDWEEK Return Fare **4/-**
	AT 4.15pm	**Single trip to Greenwich & London** Ample time to return by train to Southend.	Single Fare **6/-**
Friday **20th** September	**AT 12.15pm** Returning App: 6.30pm	**Day return to HERNE BAY** Allowing over 2 hours ashore. Passengers may also remain on board for special cruise from Herne Bay.	Day Return **ONLY 9/6** Inc: Sea Cruise **14/-**
	AT 6.30pm	**Single trip to GRAVESEND** Ample time to return by train & ferry to Southend.	Single Fare **4/6**
Saturday **21st** September	**2.35pm** Returning App: 3.40pm	**Afternoon Sea Cruise** Around the Estuaries of the Thames & Medway	Return Fare **4/-**
	AT 3.45pm	**Single Trip to Greenwich & London** Ample time to return by train to Southend.	Single Fare **6/-**
Final Sailings Sunday **22nd** September	**2.35pm** Returning App: 4.15pm	**Afternoon Sea Cruise** Up the Thames & over to the Medway to view Allhallows Canvey Island Shellhaven etc:	SPECIAL Return Fare **5/-**
	AT 4.15pm	**Single trip to Greenwich & London** Ample time to return by train to Southend.	Single Fare **6/-**

All sailings subject to weather & circumstances permitting. Passengers are only carried on the terms & conditions printed on the back of the ticket.   Tickets available on the Steamer and in advance from:- 144 Sumner Rd. S.E.15 BER 3480   REDUCED FARE CHILDREN UNDER 14.

Handbill for the New Belle Steamers who operated *Consul* on the Thames.

The *Consul* at Greenwich Pier in September 1963. A fully laden *Royal Sovereign*, on charter, is passing at some speed on her way to the coast.

The *Consul* at Greenwich. *Consul* was very much a Victorian paddle steamer and had been built as the *Duke of Devonshire* in 1896 by R.&H. Green at Blackwall.

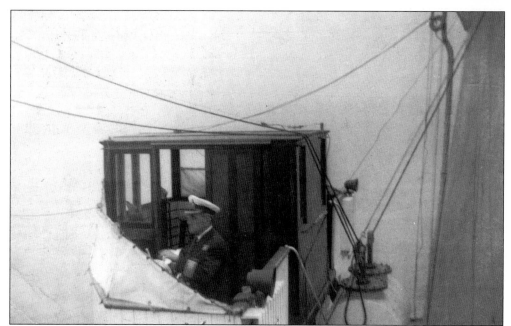

Captain Harry Defrates on the bridge of *Consul* on Sunday 22 September 1963. He was very much associated with *Consul* which he commanded in the late 1950s on the south coast. In 1963 he had *Consul* for her venture on the Sussex coast which culminated in the Thames charter.

The *Crested Eagle* had originally been built in 1938 for Scarborough services under the name of *Royal Lady*. She was purchased for service on the Thames in 1948. *Crested Eagle* took the name of the former paddle steamer lost at Dunkirk to retain possession of the name for a possible new Eagle Steamer planned for the future.

Crested Eagle is best remembered for providing the London Docks cruises, but she also undertook cruises from Tower Pier to Gravesend and Southend in the mid-1950s. She later ran cruises from Gravesend to Southend and Clacton before being placed on charter to P&A Campbell for service on the south coast but never returned to service on the Thames.

PORT OF LONDON
RIVER & DOCKS CRUISES

THROUGH THE BUSIEST REACHES OF THE RIVER THAMES AND THE ROYAL ALBERT & KING GEORGE V DOCKS
by m.v. CRESTED EAGLE *from* TOWER PIER

AFTERNOON CRUISES
LEAVING TOWER PIER at 2·30 p.m. – ARRIVING BACK at 6·15 p.m. (approx.)

EVERY SATURDAY *from the 9th. JUNE until the 15th. SEPTEMBER inclusive*	*EVERY WEDNESDAY & THURSDAY* *from the 18th. JULY until the 13th. SEPTEMBER inclusive*

MORNING CRUISES
LEAVING TOWER PIER at 9·30 a.m. – ARRIVING BACK at 1·15 p.m. (approx.)

ON THURSDAYS
26th JULY, 9th. 16th. & 30th. AUGUST

NEAREST UNDERGROUND STATION – TOWER HILL
PRIVATE CAR PARK ADJACENT TO TOWER PIER

LIGHT REFRESHMENTS OBTAINABLE ON BOARD

FARES
ADULTS 7/- JUVENILES 3/6 (under 16 years of age)

ADVANCE BOOKINGS
APPLY – CHIEF INFORMATION OFFICER (Docks Cruise Section)
PORT of LONDON AUTHORITY · TRINITY SQUARE · E·C·3
TELEPHONE · ROYAL 2000

Also bookings on Tower Pier on day of cruise from 9 a.m. for Morning Cruises and 1·30 p.m. for Afternoon Cruises

Printed & Published by the Port of London Authority, Trinity Sq. E.C.3

Crested Eagle was sold to Maltese interests in 1957 and renamed *Imperial Eagle*. She operated out of Gozo until being scrapped in November 1994. She is seen here lying derelict in Valetta harbour.

In 1966-1967 the Clyde favourite *Jeanie Deans* was re-named *Queen of the South* for operation on the Thames.

Queen of the South at Tilbury with proud owner Don Rose showing visitors around the ship. As well as professional workmen, many volunteers assisted in the refit.

COASTAL STEAM PACKET CO. LTD.
ROSEWAY   HOUSE . OLD   KENT   ROAD .   LONDON . S E 1

The Directors cordially invite you to join them

ON A SPECIAL

INAUGURAL CRUISE

ON BOARD

P. S. "QUEEN OF THE SOUTH"

DEPARTING FROM TOWER PIER AT

10 a.m. on THURSDAY, MAY *26th.* 1966

(ARRIVING BACK BETWEEN 4.30 AND 5.00 p.m.)

Dress : Informal
Buffet Lunch served on board

R.S.V.P.
on enclosed card
by MAY 1st. 1966

Kindly bring this invitation with you when embarking at Tower Pier.

The Coastal Steam Packet Company was a consortium headed by London grocer, Don Rose. Their fine plans included a sum of at least £40,000 spent on refurbishment that culminated in the inaugural cruise shown on this invitation. The high hopes were soon dashed as *Queen of the South* was tied up until the following Monday because of mechanical problems – a sign of things to come!

Let's cruise away for a day

New This Year
ON LONDON'S LATEST PLEASURE STEAMER

P.S. *QUEEN OF THE SOUTH*
(Largest and fastest vessel of her class in Europe)

DAILY SEA & RIVER CRUISES (Except Fridays)
TO MANY OF YOUR FAVOURITE HOLIDAY RESORTS
Regular Service Direct From
TOWER OF LONDON PIER & GREENWICH NEXT CUTTY SARK
Depart 9-30 a.m.   Depart 10 a.m.
TO
Southend - Clacton - Herne Bay
ETC.

 Avoid congestion by road and relax instead, enjoying excellent meals, fully licensed bars (open all day), dancing, bingo, music, etc., etc., with sun and fresh air on the broad river or ocean highroad all the way.

EARLY BOOKING STRONGLY ADVISED WITH
Coastal Steam Packet Co. Ltd.
ROSEWAY HOUSE, OLD KENT ROAD, S.E.I.
Tel. BER. 3480 (Also BER. 3879 from 1st May)
Please see over for full details, fares, conditions, etc.

WITH COMPLIMENTS

This brochure shows the potential that the *Queen of the South* might have had if she had not been dogged by mechanical problems. It included details to attract party organisers where a full day trip inclusive of a three-course lunch and high tea cost £1.25.

Queen of the South approaching Southend Pier. It was the intention to operate the vessel daily except Fridays, from London to Southend, Clacton or Herne Bay. Southend was of course always a favourite, and passengers who paid the 15s return fare, also had the option of a coach trip to Malden or Burnham-on-Crouch.

Disembarking passengers at Southend. Just twelve years later another Clyde favourite, the *Waverley*, would offer a carbon-copy image as she started her successful career on the Thames.

The dining saloon of the *Queen of the South* showing Don Rose along with other prominent supporters of the venture. The dining saloon had changed little since 1931 and offered a high standard of silver service catering. It was indeed a dining saloon in the finest Thames tradition where breakfast (32p), high tea (27p) and dinner were served.

Don Rose (right) talking to Capt. Tommy Aldis DSC, who had been a regular master of Queen Line Steamers and became the first master of the new *Queen of the Channel* after the Second World War. Capt. Aldis could offer a wealth of experience to the *Queen of the South* venture.

In an attempt to revive *Queen of the South*'s luck, the boiler was retubed and interiors refurbished ready for the 1967 season. The ship is seen here on her inaugural cruise on 8 June 1967. This 'cruise' consisted of being towed from Tower Pier because of yet another malfunction of machinery.

10 June 1967 was a sad day for *Queen of the South* as she was towed away to Blackwall for repairs after breaking down only two days into her season.

The *Queen of the South* offered a wide range of facilities. The Sunshine Bar on the promenade deck and cocktail bar on the main deck offered more traditional refreshment, while the dining saloon and cafeteria ensured that passengers were well fed. The soda fountain offered ices, confectionery and soft drinks while a seafood bar offered Leigh cockles, Margate shrimps and Whitstable whelks. Finally, the River Room offered passengers the chance to dance to the 'Meletrone' before finishing with a game of Bingo. Entertainment was sometimes offered by Barry Cryer who performed traditional Music Hall entertainment.

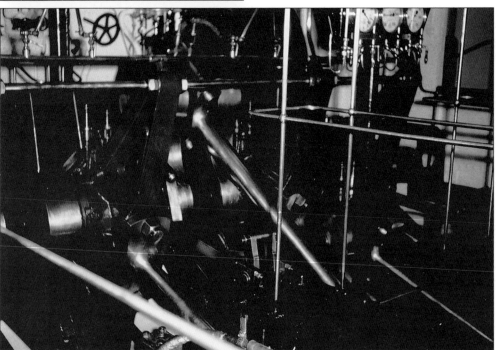

The three-crank, triple expansion engine of *Queen of the South*. Unfortunately the ship was dogged from the outset by boiler and paddle wheel failures which led to the cancellation of many cruises and, ultimately, the demise of this fine paddle steamer.

The valiant attempt to re-introduce a paddle steamer service to the Thames took a great commitment by countless supporters as well as the owners of *Queen of the South*. This handbill shows what might have been if circumstances had been different. Today, Whitstable is a favourite destination of many enthusiasts who travel on the pleasure steamers of the twenty-first century.

Queen of the South moored off Tower Pier, London. After mounting debts and a far from illustrious career on the Thames, *Queen of the South* was towed away by the tug *Dhulia* in December 1967 for scrapping at Antwerp.

QUEEN OF THE SOUTH TO BE SOLD

Eltham man's venture fails

A N Eltham business man, Mr. Donald Rose, left his Kings-orchard home for a holiday this week feeling "ill and heartbroken" after the failure of his venture with the paddle steamer Queen of the South. His doctor had ordered him to take a complete rest.

After accidents in which the paddles were damaged by driftwood, the public lost faith in the ship, and the Queen of the South has been put up for sale.

Mr. Rose and his friends had spent many thousands of pounds renovating the 35-year-old ship, formerly the Jeanie Deans, the biggest and most famous of the Clyde paddle steamers.

At Whitsun they inaugurated a day service to the Thames Estuary, which, it was hoped, would recapture the spirit of the paddle steamer trips which were so popular in pre-war days—complete with cockles, shrimps and whelks.

MOORED AT TOWER

On Tuesday the Queen of the South sailed on what could be one of her last journeys from Southend to Tower Pier, where she is now moored.

Her operators, the Coastal Steam Packet Co., hope to get more than £30,000 for the ship, and, if possible, to save her from the breaker's yard for the second time.

Mr. Rose's brother—solicitor Mr. Jack Rose—said this week the venture had failed mainly because of staff shortages and lack of public support.

"We found it impossible to get an adequate crew and catering staff. We had a number of accidents involving driftwood. These upset our sailing schedules and the public lost faith, for they could never be sure if the ship would arrive."

The Queen of the South began her day-trip service from London to the Thames Estuary at Whitsun, but twice in a fortnight the paddles were broken by driftwood.

On both occasions Mr. Donald Rose had to put his hand in his pocket and pay his passengers' fares home.

Then he paid out again to have the paddles repaired and strengthened. But it was too late—as a result of the accidents he had lost both his crew and his customers.

The sad end of a dream.

In September 1968 the Portsmouth-Ryde paddle steamer *Ryde* spent a short time on charter to Gilbey's Gin as a 'floating gin palace'. Many passengers seemed more impressed with the quality of the gin than the *Ryde*, and the few days spent on the Thames were very busy indeed with many TV personalities such as Jimmy Edwards aboard. This photograph shows the logo on the funnel along with a large array of flags flying. A brass band is also playing on the deck.

The *Queen of the Isles* arriving at Margate on Saturday 24 May 1969. After disembarking passengers, a short sea cruise was offered before returning to Southend and London.

WHITE FUNNEL FLEET

P. & A. CAMPBELL LTD.

SEASON 1969

Sailings from **London (Tower Pier)**

by the Motor Vessel "Queen of the Isles"

TO

SOUTHEND & MARGATE

on the following Saturdays

May 24; June 7, 21; July 5, 26; August 9, 23; Sept. 6

Leave Tower Pier	Arrive Southend	Arrive Margate	Leave Margate	Leave Southend	Arrive Tower Pier
9.0 a.m.	11.55 a.m.	2.35 p.m.	3.50 p.m.	6.20 p.m.	9.45 p.m.

FARES

From London to Southend	17/6 Single	22/6 Day Return
From London to Margate	22/6 Single	32/6 Day Return

(Children over three and under fourteen half price)

NOTE: On arrival at Margate the vessel makes a short sea cruise. Passengers wishing to remain on board and not disembark at Margate may do so on payment of a supplementary fare of 5/-.

THE QUEEN OF THE ISLES, built in 1964 for service between Penzance and the Isles of Scilly, upon which route she is employed during the winter, is a twin screw motor vessel of 515 tons and approximately 150 feet in length. She has comfortable accommodation for 300 passengers.

PLEASE TURN OVER FOR CONDITIONS OF CARRIAGE AND OTHER GENERAL INFORMATION

In 1969, P&A Campbell Ltd operated the *Queen of the Isles* from London to Southend and Margate on a fortnightly basis. She also undertook some cruises from Ramsgate and Margate to Ostend and Boulogne. With many light sailings to and from the South coast, this service became uneconomic and Campbell's announced that the service would not be repeated in 1970.

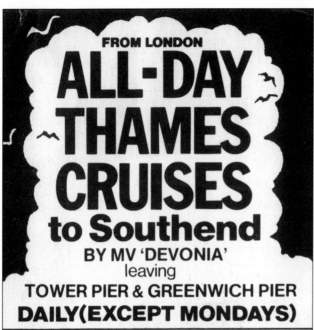

FROM LONDON

ALL-DAY THAMES CRUISES

to Southend

BY MV 'DEVONIA'
leaving
TOWER PIER & GREENWICH PIER
DAILY (EXCEPT MONDAYS)

Leave	Return
Tower Pier 10.00	Southend 16.30
Greenwich Pier 10.30	Due Greenwich 19.30
Due Southend 13.40	Tower Pier 20.00 (approx.)

Tickets obtainable at the Pier or on board.
Return fares: Adult £5.00 Child (3–14) £2.50
Single fares: Adult £3.00 Child (3–14) £1.50
Carries 600 Passengers   Snacks,
Licensed Bars, Light Refreshments

Also Available for
Private Evening Charters.
Details on request.

THAMES ESTUARY CRUISES
on Tuesdays, Wednesdays, Saturdays & Sundays

There is a cruise of approx. 1¾ hours
duration in the Thames estuary,
leaving Southend Pier at 14.30 and
due back at 16.15.
Passengers from London who
wish to remain aboard for this cruise
may do so on payment of an extra
fare of:
Adult £1.00 Child (3–14) 50p

WHITE FUNNEL FLEET

P. & A. Campbell Limited
Enquiries: Tel. 01-481-3681

The *Devonia* (ex *Scillonian*) was
placed in service on the
Thames in 1977 and was
operated by P&A Campbell
Ltd. She commenced service
on 14 July but was not a
success and transferred to the
Bristol Channel in the
following year.

Six
The Rebirth: Waverley
and her Consorts

The *Waverley* arrives at Tower Pier for the first time on 29 April 1978.

The beat of paddles finally returned to the Thames in the spring of 1978 when *Waverley* rounded Land's End for a month long season of cruises along the south coast and Thames. Here *Waverley*'s traditional 'fan board' outlines some of the destinations of this first season of cruises.

These four passengers were lucky enough to travel aboard *Waverley* on her first visit to the Thames. They left the Clyde on 15 April 1978 for the 600 mile sea voyage, each paying £100 for the privilege. They are: John Grant, Margaret Russell, Basil Craggs and Peter Stocker. They are of course all wearing the traditional *Waverley* bobble hat!

110

Waverley arriving at Tilbury on 10 May 1980 with the Gravesend to Tilbury ferry *Edith* about to disembark her passengers ahead of the paddler. *Edith* herself had offered cruises from Gravesend to Greenwich and Tower Pier on Wednesdays and Sundays in the 1960s.

On 28 April 1978, *Waverley*, on a charter in the River Medway, lost her anchor whilst swinging below Rochester Bridge. However the anchor was retrieved by the local vessel *Medway Otter* and taken to Southend. This photograph shows the anchor being restored to *Waverley* on the following day.

A photograph confirming that *Waverley* had arrived in London on 29 April 1978.

Waverley's gangway is positioned at Deal. There is a good queue of passengers waiting on the pier about to board the paddler.

It is now 2.45 p.m. and *Waverley* has embarked her passengers at Deal for a cruise around the Goodwin Sands on a glorious summer's day.

Waverley passes the Royal Naval College at Greenwich, *c.*1980.

The *Waverley* approaching Southend Pier during her first season on the Thames. The wreck of the Mulberry harbour section can be seen to the left of the vessel.

Waverley departing on a charter for Penguin Books on 20 September 1986.

Waverley alongside Southend Pier, *c.*1985.

On 12 May 1980, the *Waverley* took part in an emotional wreath laying ceremony by Capt. John Cameron off the French coast to mark the fortieth anniversary of the Dunkirk evacuation. Capt. Cameron commanded the *Waverley* of 1899 sunk during the evacuation and was the first master of the present *Waverley* in 1947.

On 27 May 1990, Waverley followed the Dunkirk little ships across the English Channel to commemorate the Dunkirk evacuation. On a beautiful sunny day, she returned to Ramsgate amongst a sea of little ships and tied up to see them all parade into the harbour for perhaps the last time.

Observed from the stern of *Waverley*, the sun sets between the incomplete structure of the Queen Elizabeth II Bridge at Dartford, c.1989.

Waverley at the Prince of Wales Pier, Dover, on 24 September 1989. She had just arrived with passengers from Ramsgate.

Waverley's crew photographed on the Clyde in 1997. In the second row are Kenneth Henderson (Chief Engineer), Capt. Graeme Gellatly (*Waverley's* present Master), Capt. Steve Michel, Jim McFadzean (Purser) with Craig Peacock (Catering Officer) in the bottom right hand corner.

An aerial view of the *Waverley* passing under the Orwell Bridge, Ipswich, on 5 October 1999 on a cruise to London.

The *Kingswear Castle* about to arrive back at London Bridge City Pier on one of her annual visits to London. The *Kingswear Castle* was built for service on the River Dart in Devon in 1924. After a long period of restoration, she re-entered service on the Medway and Thames in 1985 under the command of Capt. John Megoran. *Kingswear Castle* offers the enthusiast the unique experience of a cruise on the Thames aboard a traditional coal-fired paddle steamer.

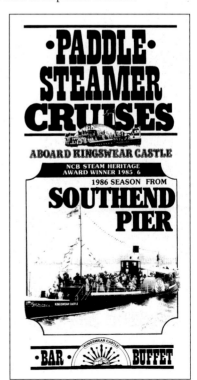

This *Kingswear Castle* brochure from 1986 lists cruises from Southend Pier. During 1986, *Kingswear Castle* undertook one hour cruises on Wednesdays, Thursdays and Saturdays from the Pier Head.

A paddle steamer photograph for the twenty-first century. *Kingswear Castle* is able to cruise further up the Thames than her famous consorts. On this special cruise in September 2000, *Kingswear Castle* undertook a charter that took her to a new London landmark, the London Eye.

The annual trip to London has become a firm favourite of *Kingswear Castle* supporters since she re-entered service. In the early days the vessel ran cruises for the Gravesham Edwardian Fair. Here *Kingswear Castle* has just arrived at London in June 1987.

The *Balmoral* approaching Margate in June 2000. Although the pier has long since vanished, passengers are still able, on rare occasions, to take a traditional cruise from the old stone jetty.

Waverley passes the Millennium Dome. Despite widespread criticism, the Dome is a popular landmark for passengers to see on the trip to London. Several calls were made at the Dome's pier in the 2000 season enabling passengers to visit the attraction.

Balmoral departs from Great Yarmouth on 29 June 2000. The *Balmoral* was built in 1949 and after a long career finally entered service as *Waverley's* consort in 1986. She made her first visit to the Thames in 1987.

A historic photograph taken on 29 June 2000 at Great Yarmouth. It shows *Balmoral* setting out on a cruise to London, passing the *Waverley* in the River Yare. From January until August 2000, *Waverley* was at Great Yarmouth for a major rebuild to painstakingly restore the ship to her 1947 condition and at the same time ensured that the ship met the stringent regulations required in the twenty first century. The results are quite astonishing.

The *Haven Cruiser* passes *Waverley* on the 4 August 2000. The hull has been rebuilt and the lines are being painted around it. The deck shelters are in the process of being 'scumbled' and the funnels await their traditional colours of red, white and black.

With just ten days to go before her first cruise, there is still a huge amount of work to be done.

With the paddle box not yet fitted, it is possible to get a good view of *Waverley*'s paddle wheel.

Waverley re-entered service on the Clyde on 18 August 2000 after a huge effort by the rebuild team to complete this major maritime project on time. After a season on the south coast, *Waverley* made her way to the Thames. Here she is seen at Whitstable in October 2000.

A highlight of any Thames season aboard *Waverley* is the cruise from Tower Pier to Tilbury and Southend for the 'Grand Parade of Steam' in the River Medway. Here *Waverley* resplendent in her 1947 livery once again, is photographed from the *Kingswear Castle* in October 2000. There seems to be not a square inch of free space on *Waverley* as passengers crowd to see the other paddle steamer.

Waverley at Tower Pier in the autumn of 2000.

The pier head at Southend in April 2001. Sadly the pier has suffered two disastrous fires since 1976 when the section of the pier to the right of this photograph was nearly destroyed. On the far left is the RNLI lifeboat station that opened in 2001. Southend Pier is still important to the pleasure steamers and there are ambitious plans to rebuild attractions on it in the future.

Waverley alongside Clacton Pier in October 2000.

There is only one way to end this book and that is with a photograph of *Waverley* set against Tower Bridge, London. For over 100 years, Tower Bridge has greeted passengers as they anticipate a day trip to the sea or is the landmark that welcomes them back home at the end of a day of pleasure. In this world of fast developing technology, this piece of Victorian engineering still delights and stirs the emotion of passengers in the same way as it did their forefathers. This is also true of *Waverley*. Under the command of Captains Graeme Gellatly and Steve Colledge, whose supreme skills and seamanship ensure that each passenger receives a happy and safe cruise, *Waverley* has recently emerged rebuilt to her 1947 glory. It is good to reflect that the long and distinguished heritage of pleasure steamers on the Thames is indeed safe and flourishing with *Waverley*, *Kingswear Castle* and *Balmoral*. Long may it continue!